for Jean

Arrival of the Queen of Sheba

(from 'Solomon')

Arranged by
WATSON FORBES

G. F. HANDEL

When the duet string versions are performed, the pianist should play the notes in small type and omit the sections in brackets.
Duration: 3 minutes

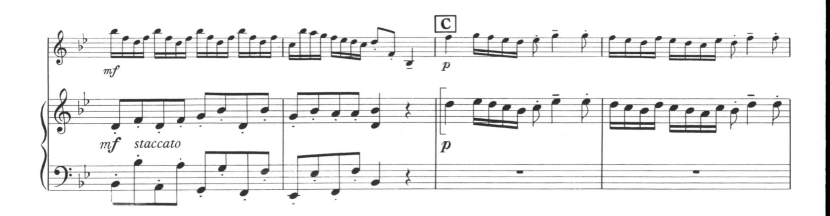

Arrival of the Queen of Sheba

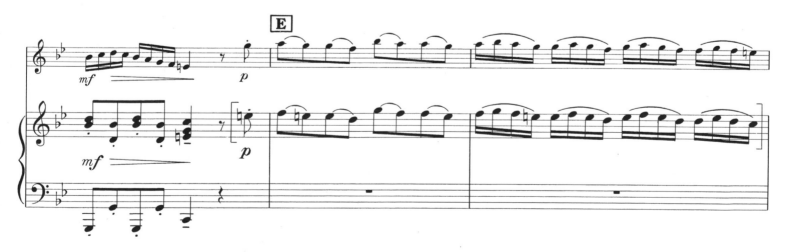

Arrival of the Queen of Sheba

4

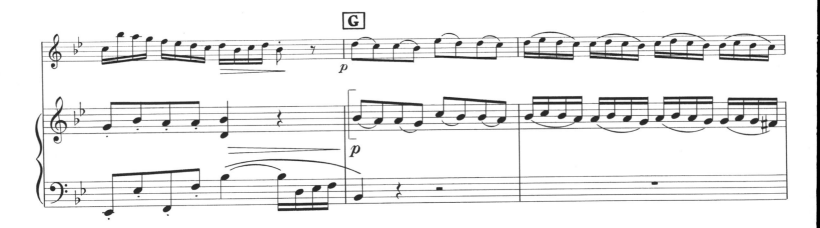

Arrival of the Queen of Sheba

Violin

Arrival of the Queen of Sheba

for Jean

Arrival of the Queen of Sheba
(from 'Solomon')

Arranged for Viola and Piano by
WATSON FORBES

G. F. HANDEL

Viola

Viola

Arrival of the Queen of Sheba

for Jean

Arrival of the Queen of Sheba
(from 'Solomon')

Arranged for Violin and Piano by
WATSON FORBES

G. F. HANDEL

Violin

Arrival of the Queen of Sheba

(from 'Solomon')

Arranged for two Violins and Piano by
WATSON FORBES

G. F. HANDEL

2nd Violin

Printed in Great Britain
OXFORD UNIVERSITY PRESS, MUSIC DEPARTMENT, GREAT CLARENDON STREET, OXFORD OX2 6DP

2nd Viola

Arrival of the Queen of Sheba

for Jean

Arrival of the Queen of Sheba

(from 'Solomon')

Arranged for two Violas and Piano
(or Violin, Viola and Piano) by
WATSON FORBES

G. F. HANDEL

2nd Viola

2nd Violin

Arrival of the Queen of Sheba

Arrival of the Queen of Sheba

6

Arrival of the Queen of Sheba

Arrival of the Queen of Sheba

Processed and printed by
Halstan & Co. Ltd., Amersham, Bucks., England

OXFORD UNIVERSITY PRESS